Sacred and Intimate Lives of Husbands *and* Wives

Blessings,
Herts Wasp
9/14/19

Sacred and Intimate Lives of Husbands and Wives

Helpful Hints on Embracing the Marriage Journey

Hertistine Washington

THIRD DAY PRESS

AN IMPRINT OF AUTHORSOURCE

Published by Third Day Press
An Imprint of AuthorSource, Inc.
www.authorsourcemedia.com

Cover and Interior Layout Design by AuthorSource, Inc.

ISBN: 978-1-947939-81-3
E-book ISBN: 978-1-947939-82-0
Library of Congress: 2019932516

Printed in the United States

The Vow of Commitment

...to have and to hold from this day forward, for better, for worse, for richer, for poorer, in sickness and in health, to love and to cherish, till death do us part, according to God's holy ordinance; and thereto I pledge thee my faith.

Dedication

*This book is dedicated with love and appreciation
to my darling husband, Harvest,
who continues to grow with me in holy matrimony,
in the knowledge and wisdom
of our Lord and Savior Jesus Christ;
and
to our four children:
Tiffany, Harvest Jr., Rosie, and Willie,
with which our union was made all the better.
To God be praised always!*

Contents

Acknowledgments

- *All glory to God for giving me the desire, energy, strength, and illumination to bring forth this work.*
- *To my loving husband, I acknowledge God for your love, patience, and care of me. I appreciate your support, input, understanding, and for providing me with much of the materials needed to write this book.*
- *To my children, I thank God for blessing our union with you. I love and appreciate you in every way.*
- *To our beautiful grandchildren, Riana, Jordan, Harvest, III, and Elahri; grateful for your smiles and enthusiasm, and always encouraging me with your love and hugs.*
- *To my church family (The Mt. Sinai Church; www. Sinai.church), I love and adore you. Thank you for your warmth and support.*
- *I further thank God for His grace in surrounding me with dear friends, married and unmarried, and associates who willingly shared their expertise on bringing this writing from pen to paper, from script to book, from book to your hands, from your hands to your heart, and from your heart to others, to the praise and glory of God our Heavenly Father.*

- *So grateful to be a member of the Power of P.E.N.S. Christian Writer's Group, which have encouraged me through prayer, expression, networking, and support.*
- *Grateful to the AuthorSource publishing company and to Beth Lottig, who has patiently guided me in bringing this work forth.*
- *Last, but not least, grateful for my late mother and father, Levi and Rosie Lee Ford, who raised me to love, respect and honor God.*

Foreword

To those who may become a reader of this marvelous book, *Sacred and Intimate Lives of Husbands and Wives,* I say to you, your marriage and your life will be better for it. I am the long-time thankful and blessed husband of one, Hertistine Washington. Even as kids growing up, Hertistine (well known as Kitty, and to others later in life as Miss Kitty), has been doing some form of writing: taking notes, writing reminders, poems, special information, short stories, and letters, which some I still have today. Also, she loves jotting down daily and future events coming up. Just to say, she has been continually writing in some manner, resulting in books all along; which she nor I knew was going to happen.

I grew up and around Hertistine. I first saw her when I was 17 and she was 14. The principal of my high school had chosen me to supervise the study hall, and to write down the names of all who were talking and not studying. There Hertistine was, sitting in the bleachers of the gym, talking and not studying. I knew then, that her name was the *one name* I was not going to write down. That was the day I really, really noticed my wife to be. That special moment in time began our courtship of love that has lasted a life time.

My beautiful wife has a deep love for God, family,

friends, elder people, and love for people altogether. Now through all these years, I am grateful to God for giving me a wife fit for me that loves Him more than me. I thank Him for His mercy that keeps us loving. So, to her and our surprise, here it is, *Sacred and Intimate Lives of Husbands and Wives*. It is one that tells of God's design for marriage, and how to pursue a marriage His way.

I pray that this book takes off with eagle's wings, and be as peaceful doves in people lives.

Her grateful husband,
Harvest

Introduction

I can't express how grateful I am to God for putting this book in my heart, *Sacred and Intimate Lives of Husbands and Wives,* which provides helpful hints on embracing the marriage journey. My husband Harvest and I thank God for what we have learned, and still learning every day in a new way. We are ever-coming to the knowledge of what this great institution holds. I can't begin to enumerate the mistakes we've made on this marriage journey; definitely, too many to count. Some we will share, but others are only for God's ear.

This book, however, is not about the mistakes which happened in our marriage, or any marriage for that matter. Rather, it's about becoming awakened to the sovereignty of God within a marriage; bringing to light His authority, control, and guidance within a union; generating an awareness of His wisdom on how to maintain a loving, caring, and supportive marriage that will be fulfilling, and God glorifying at the same time; and encouraging couples to pursue their marriage according to God's design, in hopes of building one that will be a powerful expression of His love and purpose.

At the onset of writing this book, we would have been married one month shy of 42 years. We've learned, it doesn't matter how many years anyone has been married, no amount of years is enough to produce an expert. Let me be clear, I don't profess to be an expert on marriage, only a blessed experienced participant of God's grace and mercy. I still welcome any spiritual wisdom on this subject.

I've come to realize marriage is a covenant, a sacred institution, and an intimate union that can never be sustained by fleshly experts. It requires constant spiritual attention and intervention from a higher source than on earth. So, if you're looking for your spouse to be that expert, cut it out; stop it. He nor she is perfect and never will be. There are no marital experts in the flesh that can maintain, make happy, or *fix* a marriage. There is only one expert who has never sinned and never married. His name is Jesus. He has provided a sacred plan that will keep a marriage loving, surviving, and thriving. This plan can be found in His holy book, the Bible. In it, you will find God's heart and design on how to embrace this sacred and intimate union.

How This Book Came About

One early morning (November 10, 2017), as my husband and I were having some kind of disagreement, and both feeling some kind-da way, I shouted: *"Oh, the lives of husbands and wives!!!"* After taking a deep breath, I again cried out, "Lord, help us!" Yes, my dear sweet husband, right at 42 years of marriage, whom I love and adore, had pushed an unexpected button in me that early morning... and it was buzzing really loud! No one's fault in particular. It was just one of those mornings! Maybe you can relate?

Yes, we are both Christians and love the Lord Jesus. But sometimes, I must confess, those unforeseen moments fly in like a rocket to disturb the peace we both share in Christ, and we react! After realizing we weren't at ourselves, we quickly acknowledged our behavior. That day, standing in the kitchen, we paused and prayed for forgiveness. After which, we went about our day with no hurt feelings. I assure you, at the beginning of our marriage, we weren't always so spontaneous to recognize when we had allowed the enemy to creep in. Being human, sometimes we still get caught off guard, but not as much.

A few minutes after admitting our behavior, I continued to think on the topic, *Lives of Husbands and Wives.* My mind reflected on a conversation I had with a dear sister-friend who once said to me, "Sometimes God will just download something in your spirit." Un-beknowing, (in that disagreeable/yet repentance moment, that's what I believe He did). So much was pouring into my mind on *Lives of Husbands and Wives,* I began texting those thoughts to myself.

After settling into a moment of stillness, I was moved to add, *Sacred Lives of Husbands and Wives.* I knew then, this was that "something" my friend shared with me earlier. I believe it came from the very heart of God, but not until I confessed. On receiving the download, I was able to upload to, *Sacred and Intimate Lives of Husbands and Wives: helpful hints on embracing the marriage journey.*

CHAPTER 1

Embracing the Awakening

*W*ouldn't you say, to wake up is the best thing? Especially, to be awakened from darkness to light is an amazing moment! Your heart overflows with gratitude that your eyes became opened, and now you could see! How wonderful is that? This is why I entitled my first chapter, "Embracing the Awakening." For that's the way I felt when my eyes became opened to the sovereignty of God in our marriage. One of my favorite scriptures I often pray is, Lord, "Open my eyes, that I may behold wondrous things out of your law" (Psalm 119:18). Needless to say, when God opens your eyes, it's a wonderful awakening!

Before my husband and I could fully embrace our marriage, we had to first be awakened to the sacredness and intimacy this great union holds. We needed to come to the awareness of what it was about; better still, "who" this union "is" about. Then and only then were we able to embrace this glorious awakening.

1

Initially, we went into marriage with the mindset that *"weee's loooveees each other,"* and that was what mattered most. As long as I knew that my love loved me, I was okay, and I believed so was he. Now after many years of marriage, our eyes have come opened to seeing things in a different way; (1) our *love* wasn't enough and (2) our *marriage* has a higher purpose than just about us.

We both were raised in large Christian families, and lived on separate plantations in the Mississippi Delta, where we enjoyed the outdoors and country life. As teenagers, we also worked on these plantations; chopping and picking cotton, beans, and corn. Living a few miles from each other, it's not surprising, we attended the same high school. It was there, we found each other. Allow me to re-phrase, there, God connected us together for his divine purpose—cause' we weren't looking. Now—there we were, in our kitchen, right at 42 years of marriage, having one of those crazy disagreeable moments that maybe only a seasoned godly married couple might understand.

In the Beginning: The Missing Link

When we first got married, we didn't think of our marriage as being about God, His love and purpose. We never spoke about it in that fashion. We thought marriage was about *our* love and *our* purpose for *our* marriage. All we wanted was to get married, have a house, and one day have some children (We were "in love" with each other). We hadn't considered we should love God more than ourselves and our union. Later we found that our love wasn't enough; it "alone" wasn't strong enough to support our marriage, especially in a God-designed way. Though we didn't separate, our marriage became too heavy for ourselves. When this began to happen, we realized something was missing. Today, we know it wasn't something, but *someone.*

Although we had accepted Christ as our Savior, and became faithful attenders at church, we did not let that *someone* have their rightful position—Lord of our life and marriage. We had neglected to allow Him to be the front, head, and center of our union. I admit, we weren't living a Spirit filled life in Him, as we thought.

Yes, we prayed, praised, read our Bible, jumped and shouted, and were in church most Sundays. We also attended Sunday School with our children and midweek Bible class. Yet, at the same time, doing what most young couples did to have fun in the world; partied on Saturday night, and in church on Sunday morning. You get the picture? We were living for ourselves while playing both sides of the spiritual fence. We had a zeal for God, but not according to knowledge. While we were being faithful to each other, we were not being faithful to God. As in the book of Joshua 24:15, a decision needed to be made: "And if it is evil in your eyes to serve the LORD, choose this day whom you will serve... But as for me and my house, we will serve the LORD." We had to make a decision to continue to serve our fleshly pleasures, or to serve God.

I tell you, it took a while before we embraced that concept. Truth be told, years later with four children underfoot. As I look back, I thank God for His ever-present mercy during those years! We're grateful He has kept us together long enough for it to register that our marriage was not all about us, nor our four children.

So, as we tried to make our union work effectively, a void certainly had remained. *Someone* was indeed missing. As time went by, we came to know that it was God; He was the missing link. Even though we still loved each other as much as ever, we now embrace loving in a new and different way. We are no longer looking to ourselves for that ultimate "loving" feeling; we look to God. Still, before we could fully embrace this sacred union, we needed more light and insight, as we were to travel several foggy roads.

My Party Time

One day something added to that missing link feeling in our marriage. Years earlier, as a preschool teacher, I had experienced a back injury. It happened during recess when one of my beautiful little darlings (accidentally) kicked a ball into my lower back. "What else could possibly happen?" I thought. Well, my doctor took me off work for eight months, which felt like an eternity! So, since I was off work, I decided to have a party every day—a *pity party.*

During that time, I was determined to nurse and focus on the three P's in my life (and it wasn't, prayer, patience, or perseverance), but my *pain,* my *problem,* and my *predicament;* they took priority. It seemed that nothing else mattered. Little did I know, God was getting ready to open my eyes to who I was and who He is. Having to sit back and think (uh, you guessed it), I had *time.*

Besides teaching, my job had also consisted of writing and documenting children's behavior. Now that I was at home (alone), I figured it was time for me to do the same on myself. At first, I wrote about everything that was happening to me that involved my pain, problem, and predicament. But when I got sick and tired, of being "tired and sick" of writing about myself (since I was a Christian), I started back occasionally reading God's Word. Now, the more I read, the more I wanted to read. The more I would read, the more I began to meditate. Finally, God had my attention. During my meditation I became convicted that I wasn't the wife nor *Christian* I thought I was. God began showing me "me" in ways I had never seen myself. And yes, He's still working on me.

Although I never thought of myself as a self-absorbed person, I admit I had become a little selfish in my marriage in a *quiet-cute-kinda* way; pouting when I got upset, holding back on some things, and literally unresponsive at times. Looking back, that really wasn't very cute. I didn't realize I had this strong will to have it my way, or there would be a problem in LA. My husband often matched my will. So, there we were, two peas in a pod, with no help seemingly in sight. Nonetheless, I thank God (in spite of) my husband didn't waver in picking up the pieces while I was in party mode. He continued to wait on me hand and foot, worked, cooked, and made sure the kids got to school on time. I now know it was only God giving him the strength and patience to do so and bear up with me. Yet, while he continued to carry on, I had become a pitiful mess wallowing alone in myself.

Me, Controlling?

I must also confess, while indulging in self-pity, I became a bit controlling, to say the least. Honestly, I wasn't sure if I wanted to include this segment in my book. Then I thought, it may encourage spouses to observe how they really interact with one another; it was an eye opener for me. In fact, especially in marriage, couples need to be watchful for this unwanted and most damaging invasion— *the control invasion*. It can creep in before you know it. If this segment blesses you, then it was all worth sharing.

It happened that during the time of my pity party my mom got sick and everyone journeyed back home, my family included. We've always been a close-knit family, once consisting of seven brothers and five sisters. Needless to say, when family members get together, there are many observations and interactions that take place. I'm grateful that most of the time, we had pretty good gatherings. But this time, something was deeply puzzling me.

Finally, the day came that our mom got better, and we were ecstatic! We could now leave for our own homes. My two younger sisters, and my immediate family were the last to leave. Just before they left, my youngest sister seemed to purposely position herself on a sofa chair across from me; she was not talking. This was strange because she and I usually filled our time chatting and laughing. Not at that moment, however, she was engaged in writing. As much as I wanted to know what she was writing, I didn't ask. But I did notice (every now and then), she would pause and looked in my direction, not saying a word.

Since we hadn't had any differences or misunderstandings, I couldn't help but think, "What is she writing? Is she writing to me?" Sure enough, when she got up to leave, she handed me a letter with instructions not to read until I get back to LA. "Darn it!" I thought, "She was writing to me!" It was difficult to do what she had asked, but with grinded teeth, I did.

On arriving back home, I couldn't wait to get alone in my pity party corner and read her letter. When I did, it was the sweetest most endearing letter that I wasn't ready to read. It was a letter on "control." Simply put, my sweet little sister told me in uncertain terms, I was controlling toward my husband. Now—I was upset! To make matters worse, she wasn't there so I could express how upset I was! That made me more upset. *Me, controlling?* How could she dare say that of and to *me*? I was sweet and kind to my husband (I thought). I was the one laid off work, helpless because of an injury, and still managed to fly back home to see about mom. How could I be labelled controlling? As time passed—her words didn't. The words of her letter lingered in my head like a bad headache. Still, it caused me to seriously start paying attention on how I was really interacting with my husband.

One day while reading God's Word (I can't explain it) my eyes became opened to my subtle and controlling behavior. I remember asking (no, pretty much "demanded") him to do something. Today, I don't remember exactly what that was, but I knew he humbly did it. Then like a flashing light, it registered that my sister was right. (No . . . nothing came down from heaven and hit me in the head; it was strictly from prayerfully reading and from the illuminating power of God's Word); that's what opened my eyes). I had permitted the spirit of control to invade my soul all the way to Mississippi and back to LA. It had crept in on me while I was having my pity party (*or...* maybe before). Anyway, I realized I had been using my situation to control my spouse, and someone had recognized it over 2000 miles away. Beware, husbands and wives, you may not see your controlling demanding behavior, but someone else can.

I ask, are you controlling in your marriage? If you are, will you raise your hand? No one has to see it but you and God. In all honesty, most of us have yet to meet the person who proudly acknowledges being a controlling individual; chances are, they may not even know it. But when God opens a person eyes, being controlling is definitely something not to be proud of. If you did raise your hand, I respect your honesty, and I hope you will pray to break that chain of control.

Today, I thank God for giving my sister that spiritual insight, and the courage to write a letter I very much needed to read. It helped changed my relationship with my husband. After God had done the work in my heart, I was able to call, confess, and thank her for being so loving and caring toward me and my marriage. To this day, I still have that letter to remind me of God's amazing awakening by His grace.

A Welcomed Change

As marriages do, ours also face challenges. *As soles come with shoes, challenges come with being married; it's a given.* But despite it all, we welcome God's intervention, recognizing that with His help we can overcome. I say to you, though initially, we were <u>going</u> to church, we were <u>not growing</u> in Christ. We were looking for most things from each other, which wasn't working out. Only through God's infinite mercy, were we sustained. Slowly but surely, we were beginning to embrace the awakening of *who* was in control, *who* was keeping our marriage together, and *who* our marriage was for—not us, but Him.

I can't say it enough, thanks be to God for the power of His Word. It will open eyes. It did mines. Like most pity parties, that one came to an end. After which, I made a conscious decision to read God's Word often. It brought me out of that slump, and got me back on my feet, literally and spiritually. Still, I had a lot of growing to do, but the change was coming. God was blessing me with a new way of thinking and writing. Instead of writing and focusing on me (my pain, problem, and predicament), I began writing affirmations of thanksgiving to God, which I complied in a book, *"Something to Thank About from A to Z." xulonpress.com.*

In spite of my 3 P's, God had surprised me. He had given me joy and a purpose. I never expected being at home alone with Him was going to be the best time of my day. That's when my focus, life, and marriage began to change course; God was changing me. He was waking me up, and I was happy to be awake. He was changing my pity party into a prayer and praise party, which continues today.

I want you to know, marriage is a delicate gift from God. Like any gift from Him, it is precious. It is to be held as a valuable treasure; not to be stored up, looked at, and admired as on a pedestal; also not to be misused, but to be used for His purpose and glory. It is also to be treated with godly love and godly respect for Him and toward you both.

Since we have been given this priceless gift, let us unwrap and use it to demonstrate the blessedness found in holy matrimony; a gift given to be used in time and not in eternity. As the scripture says in Matthew 22:30: "For in the resurrection they neither marry nor are given in marriage, but are like angels in heaven." Therefore, husbands and wives, do all you can in time to make your marriage shine for Him. As Jesus said: "In the same way, let your light shine before others, so that they may see your good works and give glory to your Father who is in heaven" (Matthew 5:16).

CHAPTER 2

Embracing the Sacredness of Marriage

hen I speak of the sacredness of marriage, I'm referring to that which is holy and godly. God is Holy. To embrace Him is to embrace the very One who instituted marriage in the first place. The Bibles affirms in Genesis 2:18: "Then the LORD God said: "It's not good that the man should be alone; I will make him a helper fit for him." When God said, "I will make," it is clear that He started this union off with Himself; He is the Originator; He "is" the sacredness in the union; and He united the man and woman to live in holiness together with Him and with each other. 1 Peter 1:15 tells us "but as he who called you is holy, you also be holy in all your conduct."

My husband and I have learned, since God put our union together, He desires to be in it; not only when there are challenges, but also to abide and be involved up front.

Do you know God also desires to be *in* your marriage? He wants to be an active participant, not a visitor. Are you also aware, as close as you and your spouse are, God would love to be closer? It's not enough to embrace your spouse; God wants to be embraced far more. He would love to be consulted about the things on your heart. Although He knows what you need, He has everything to offer—Himself. Jesus said in John 15:7: "If you abide in me, and my words abide in you, ask whatever you wish, and it will be done for you."

The pivotal moment in our marriage came when we started realizing it was crucial to acknowledge, honor, and give God *His* place in our union. Being that it has been many years, that moment is difficult to pinpoint. All I know is, when we stopped trying to figure our marriage out (and each other), and began seeking God as our source of help, our marriage changed. As forestated, His position is front, head, and center. Now we realize, giving Christ the Authority in our marriage, we can't lose and neither will you. I'm not saying there won't be blue days sometimes, but they'll not stay blue because of the depth of love God has for you; He's there to be your guide.

Although I'm aware there is no scientific formula that will keep a marriage working or happily together, I decided to do a little research: I asked 40 married couples, regardless of years married, faith, age, creed, or color, what is one of the main ingredients that holds their marriage together; what makes it work? Here are the majority of the answers given: "*laughter,*" "*prayer,*" "*letting my spouse be who they are; (i.e., not trying to re-invent or make over my mate),*" "*compromise,*" "*respect,*" "*trust,*" "*understanding,*" "*going with the flow—whatever comes just go with it,*" "*Jesus,*" "*listening,*" "*communication,*" "*honesty,*" "*financial awareness,*" "*patience,*" and "*love.*"

Of this survey, 75% of couples shared that knowing and depending on Jesus has sustained them; that it is He who brings the joy and stability to their union. From this simple survey, I hope you will conclude that including God in your marriage can make all the difference in the world; He can keep your union steady and strong. As yeast is the main ingredient used to make dough rise, I encourage you to let God be the main ingredient that makes your union rise in oneness, joy, love, respect, and glory to His name.

My husband and I are also becoming aware that trying to live in a marriage without godliness is far worse than trying to walk through life wearing shoes on the wrong foot. Who wants to do that? Walking like this can be most miserable. The toes can become tender and sore from being squeezed too tight. That's how one might feel when Christ is not embraced by both spouses in the marriage—squeezed and in the wrong place. Even though walking is possible, the feet could never feel just right, making one more apt to stumbling and falling. But if you both embrace God's way of walking, there's a great possibility that when you stumble, you can get back on your feet, in hopes that every further step be influenced by God's guidance. Like pre-kindergarteners (through trial and err), eventually, you hope to keep your shoes on the right foot.

The First Union

Without a doubt, God intended the lives of husbands and wives to not only be lived physically but sacredly. Indeed, the first union was established by Him. He created man in His own image, male and female. Genesis 1:27 says: "So God created man in his own image, in the image of God he created him; male and female he created them."

Knowing that man was created by the one and only Sacred God, let us strive to live in holy matrimony with each other and with Him.

Being married many years, we understand that this union absolutely requires the One who created it—God. He is GREATER, BIGGER, SMARTER, and WISER than any of us. He's in a category all by Himself. Yet, He knows all the ins and outs, and ups and downs of marriage. We believe by letting Him spear-head our marriage will cause it to function in the way it was meant to be. We hope you will reach that same conclusion.

Being that the first union was created perfectly by the perfect God, it didn't end perfectly; something went terribly wrong. After God laid the ground work, i.e., He formed man (Adam) and placed him in a beautiful garden. A little while later, God saw that it was not good for man to be alone: "Then the LORD God said: 'It is not good that the man should be alone; I will make him a helper fit for him' " (Genesis 2:18). From the rib of Adam, God gave him a helpmeet (Eve). Adam called her "woman" because she was taken from man. Now the two became one.

Now that God had established this perfect union, and provided all the Garden's amenities for living, He only had one restriction/one ground rule: "but of the tree of the knowledge of good and evil you shall not eat…," (Genesis 2:17a). One way to apply this to married life is to realize, God knew this holy union required limits. There must be rules: Do this; don't do that. Please note, husbands and wives, there are boundaries in marriage; it's not advisable to do whatever you feel like doing whenever you feel like doing it. God's way of marriage was never intended for man or woman to act independently of each other, but as one. Certainly, it was never designed to live and act apart from God. If you are a good Bible student, you know the story; you know what went wrong in the first union, man broke the rule. Man sinned, causing him to fall (Genesis 3). Beware, husbands and wives, sin will not only make you slip; it can make you fall.

Thankful, The Fall Was Not All

As we noticed in the Garden of Eden, God demanded respect for His rule. In light of man's disobedience and lack of respect for God's rule, he lost all that God had freely given him. Just as our children break our rules and we instill consequences, so did God. Because of man's sin, to the woman God said: "I will surely multiply your pain in childbearing; in pain you shall bring forth children. Your desire shall be contrary to your husband, but he shall rule over you" (Genesis 3:16). Be it known, husbands, God doesn't mean for you to "lord over" or "dominate" your wife, as if she is insignificant. Just as Christ, who is head of the Church, loves, protects, provides, nourishes, and cares for it, so are you to do for your wife, as head of your union. And to the man, God said: "By the sweat of your face you shall eat bread, till you return to the ground, for out of it you were taken; for you are dust, and to dust you shall return" (Genesis 3:19).

As a result, the Bible tells us that the man and the woman were put out of the Garden (their home), and could not re-enter. Genesis 3:24 says: "He drove out the man, and at the east of the garden of Eden he placed the cherubim and a flaming sword that turned every way to guard the way to the tree of life." What kept man from re-entering? His sin. All spiritual communication and fellowship between him and God were broken; man had fallen. Some may shrug their shoulders and say, "Oh well… that's the way the story goes." But we, who know the "Holy Story" can say, "Thank God, that's not the way the story ends!" It goes on to tell us that "God so loved the world that he gave His only begotten Son, that whosoever believeth in him should not perish, but have everlasting life" (John 3:16 KJV).

From this, we can declare that through God's infinite love and mercy, this is how the story goes: Jesus came and suffered by taking upon Himself the sin that put man out of fellowship with God. He died on the cross, and rose again that man may be forgiven and live again in constant fellowship and communion with Him. Not only that, Jesus is coming back again. By shedding His "Blood" and rising from the dead in victory, He made it possible for man to also get back up again. In light of this, let's praise God for what He has done, is doing, and what He will do through Jesus Christ the Lord—thanking Him, the Fall was not all.

Don't Be Fooled

Let us never forget, being a child of God in a Christian marriage, Satan, our adversary, is still going "to and fro" seeking whom he can devour (1 Peter 5:8 KJV). He's definitely after the marriage that desires to live for God. In lieu of this, I hope you will keep your guards up. Don't be fooled and get relaxed in thinking your marriage is solid (i.e., *you* got this). If someone say to you, "Wow, since you've made it this far, it should be smooth sailing from now on; you can eat, drink and be merry!" I beg you, don't' be fooled; that's what the devil would love for you to believe. He's secretly plotting how to tear your union apart before it gets started.

I will never forget the day prior to my husband and I getting married. Before I knew what was happening, I called the wedding off! This was due to nerves, or some other silliness stirred up from the devil. Thanks be to God, we got married on schedule. I tell you, the devil didn't want our marriage to begin or succeed, neither yours. If he could, he would blow it in pieces from the very beginning with the smallest things. Remember, he's the enemy; it is not your spouse. The Apostle Paul alerts us in Ephesians 6:12: "For we do not wrestle against flesh and blood, but against the rulers, against the authorities, against the cosmic powers over this present darkness, against the spiritual forces of evil in the heavenly places." Don't be fooled; know your foe.

Also, don't be fooled or misunderstood, sacredness in marriage doesn't mean there won't be disagreements, disappointments, failures, misunderstanding, or even hurt feelings at times. 2 Timothy 3:12 reminds us: "Indeed, all who desire to live a godly life in Christ Jesus will be persecuted." That is to say, a sacred marriage is not exempt from things that plague or war against all marriages. Quite the contrary, the godly married couples might find themselves having to stand against opposition more often than most, whether in the home or outside the home. The difference being, they have God to look to ... in order to get through.

Remember, a godly marriage reflects God's love, grace, mercy, strength, and forgiveness. The devil doesn't want any part of that. In a marriage that desires to embrace the sacredness of their union, these qualities are evident despite impending struggles. Also, husbands and wives, when you say I do, know that Satan is already waiting on you. He's not there to bring life to your marriage, but to kill, steal, and destroy it, if you let him. From the first promised vow of "I do" (and everything afterwards), will require God's attention and intervention. Don't be fooled; you cannot be happily married by yourself.

I'm aware most couples hope to begin their marriage with an elaborate ceremony of pomp and circumstance, wearing an exquisite wedding gown and the debonair tux. I encourage you both (before you dress so eloquently), first put on the whole armor of God. For it is God's Word that admonishes: "Therefore take up the whole armor of God, that you may be able to withstand in the evil day, and having done all, to stand firm" (Ephesians 6:13). Don't' be fooled; you need the armor of God to stand against the many tricks of the enemy, which will inevitably come against your holy union.

So . . . don't let the devil fool you into thinking you're "only" preparing to get your long-awaited night on. Actually, you're getting ready to get your life-long fight on with the many unseen attacks of the enemy. I don't say this to discourage any of you, but to encourage you. Don't worry or fret; you can still have victory and joy. If *you both* allow God to be the head of your union, He will sustain you. He will give patience when you need patience, and He will give strength to forgive when you submit to His will. Hopefully, you will go ahead and enjoy your blissful night, knowing that God is right there covering you with His divine love, strength, and protection. But don't be fooled—still watch and pray.

The War of the Wills

Husbands and wives, have you ever fought with your spouse? I'm not referring to a physical fist fight (... Oops!).

I'm speaking in terms of a spiritual fight. Surely, we can agree, it's not good to fight at all; it can be hurtful. Yet, many times, if we're not careful, we can find ourselves battling. Please pray to be aware of these potential encounters. They can slip in without notice and cause turmoil within your sacred union.

Therefore, be on the alert, spouses, the war has begun. There was war in heaven and war in the Garden of Eden. There are wars in the world today. Unfortunately, wars can rise up in the home of a sacred and loving marriage. Notice in James 4:1: "What causes quarrels and what causes fights among you? Is it not this, that your passions are at war within you?" Still, husbands and wives, there is something you can do. Don't sit on the sidelines. Equip yourselves with the Word of God, and take control over your passions. If you're going to fight, fight in the strength of Christ for your marriage and not against it. Know that you are not warring against each other, but the devil and his devices. I pray you and your spouse will join in Christ as a united front against the enemy.

This is spiritual warfare. In marriage, it takes two, <u>God</u> as Head, <u>you and your spouse</u> as one. Ecclesiastes 4:12 states: "And though a man might prevail against one who is alone, two will withstand him—a threefold cord is not quickly broken." Please understand, husbands and wives, God is not at war with the devil; you are. God has already won! So, get your sword (The Word) and get ready for the battle; our Lord will fight for you. He's ready in His position; now you must find yours. Permit me to give you a heads up, praying and seeking God is a great place begin.

In the early years of our marriage, Satan's attacks came unexpectedly. We allowed them to sneaked in by the way of our stubborn wills. We didn't know how strong-willed we were, until shortly after we said I do. Many times, the I do turned into "I won't," and "you better not." Un-aware to us, warring with our wills was a clever and undercover attack of the enemy (that old devil). We ignorantly permitted him to use our wills against each other.

I remember how the will wars would sometimes pop up on Saturday nights, but mostly on Sunday mornings, as we were preparing for worship. (I believe that's when the devil gets his busiest!) Sometimes out of the blue, we would find ourselves engaged in a battle of the wills. They would arise from just about anything: a mis-spoken word, getting dressed, food, toothpaste, children, a phone call, traffic, the time; you name it, it didn't matter. We hadn't realized, we had allowed Satan to come in and take our focus and our joy from what mattered most— readying our hearts for praise and worship. Instead, a silly misunderstanding had set one of us off. Please beware, and don't let that happen to you.

Also be mindful our wills count only when it's in subjection to God's will. To embrace the sacredness of this marriage union, it's essential that couples pray to humble themselves under the mighty hand of God: "Do nothing from selfish ambition or conceit, but in humility count others more significant than yourselves" (Philippians 2:3). So, be on the alert, no matter how many years you've been married, will wars can happen when you least expect it. If you're not conscious of that, you may easily find yourselves drained and fallen on the sidelines, simply because no one "chose to relinquish" their will.

We now know that Satan's goal was to take us out of "holy matrimony." More than that—to take us out—period! We're praying that as soon as one of us discern an attack of the enemy, to quickly repent to stop that attack in its track. So, husbands and wives, since the enemy will never let up, please stay on guard; if you have blinders on, please take them off; be vigilant and prayerful. Take it from us... before you find yourself engaged in a war of the wills, remember: "A soft answer turns away wrath, but a harsh word stirs up anger" (Proverbs 15:1), especially on Sunday mornings!

MADD About Marriage

Most of us are familiar with the acronym (MADD): Mothers Against Drunk Driving. Without explanation, we understand the purpose and intent: to fight against driving under the influence of alcohol because of the danger it imposes to others, as well as the drunk driver. My husband and I are also MADD. Not only in that sense, but intentionally MADD about our marriage. We are purposely pursuing and fighting for a *Marriage Against Demonic Deception:* one that's not lived under the driving influence of satanic forces. We believe if we allow these forces to overcome us, sooner or later, we can crash. Therefore, I encourage you to aim for a marriage that's not being dominated by deception.

What is demonic deception? Plainly stated, to believe a lie. It's being influenced or tricked against believing the truth. First, understand, all deception is demonic. No matter who, where, what, and how it comes, it's demonic. Think about it, who doesn't want you to know the truth? Surely, it's not God. He is Truth. There's only one other, Satan. He is the father of lies and deception. His goal is to deceive. After reading the topic, "Don't be Fooled," please permit me to share some ways we're learning to fight against demonic deception.

Since marriage is a sacred covenant instituted by
God, my husband and I are striving to maintain the mind
of Christ. If we keep our minds focused on Jesus, we are
less likely to fall captive to Satan's deception. Philippians
2:5 states: "Have this mind among yourselves, which is
yours in Christ Jesus," To have the mind of Christ is to
be mindful in the things of Christ; to be Christ-like, and
setting our affection on things above, and not on those
things of the world. It is to possess a mind that's centered
on and seeks to please the Father in truth, honesty, justice,
and love through Jesus Christ the Lord. Let us pray to
submit our minds to Him, so that we will not be easily
"under-minded" by the trickery of Satan.

Another way to fight against demonic deception is
with the Word of God. Are you aware that knowing God's
Word brings to light the kind of tricks and schemes Satan
plays? For certain, Satan has been exposed, and it is the
Word which continually exposes him. He can only hide
behind the banner of deceit if you're not aware of his
devices. Pray, read, and meditate to become wise to his
schemes. Also, pray that if you've been deceived, you'll
hurriedly repent.

Frankly speaking, we are familiar on how sly
deception can be. By talking with other spouses, here are
several scenarios we should pray to avoid: Possibly your
spouse has been late in coming home; your mind gets to
wandering... "My spouse must be somewhere he/she is not
supposed to be." Or, perhaps: You may happen to see your
spouse conversing with the opposite sex too long (in your
opinion); your mind erupts with assumptions. Another
instance: You may call your spouse on the phone and
don't get an answer. I beg you, please fight against these
thoughts, and don't react or act on them. It's a trick of the
enemy. He's trying to deceive you. He would love for you

to fill your mind with the lies of his words instead of the truth of God's Word.

I'm reminded in Hebrews 4:12: "For the word of God is living and active, sharper than any two-edged sword, piercing to the division of soul and of spirit, of joints and of marrow, and discerning the thoughts and intentions of the heart." Be confident that the Word of God is powerful enough to cut in pieces these deceptive thoughts before they take root in your mind. The Bible points out that whenever the devil tried to deceive Jesus, He would result to the Scriptures: "It is written." Colossians 3:16 also tells us to "Let the word of Christ dwell in you richly, teaching and admonishing one another in all wisdom, singing psalms and hymns and spiritual songs, with thankfulness in your hearts to God." In other words, husbands and wives, *in order to say what is written, fill your hearts with what is written.*

Again, deceitful thoughts can only enter our minds when we open the door to the deceiver—Satan, himself. God's Word keeps us informed that the devil is a trickster and not a fixer. His goal is to overthrow and bring to ruins our trust in our spouses. More so, to denounce our trust in God's provision by instilling fear. I urge you, husbands and wives, don't believe the devil's lies; that's all he has—lies. If your aim is to embrace Christ in your marriage, please guard your mind against such thoughts.

Lastly, allowing the Holy Spirit to be our guide in thought, word, and deed will ward off deceitful thinking. It is He that provides power, strength and wisdom to combat this kind of thinking by bringing to our minds what the Bible says. 2 Corinthians 10:4-5 states: "For the weapons of our warfare are not of the flesh but have divine power to destroy strongholds. We destroy arguments and every lofty opinion raised against the knowledge of God, and take every thought captive to obey Christ," In Christ, we are confident that we can take deceptive thoughts captive by enforcing the power given to us by the Holy Spirit.

Know Your Role

In order to maintain the sacredness in our marriage, my husband and I know that being aware of our roles are quite important. Therefore, we encourage each of you that God wants to use you and your marriage to be a role model for His purpose. In order for this to happen (like a good student), you must do your homework. The assignments are found in the text book of the Holy Bible. 2 Timothy 2:15a. (KJV), admonishes us to "Study to shew thyself approved unto God. . ."). Yes, husbands and wives, it's very beneficial to study what God has to say about your marriage.

By studying His Word, along with our experiences in taking tests, we find that even after many years of marriage—*we haven't passed the marriage test, nor can we*; it is Christ that does the work. We are constantly relying on Him. We are students, and by His grace we are still in school. Nonetheless, sitting under His teaching reveals what to do and what He expects in this sacred union. In His Word, the roles are clearly on display for both spouses. Although there are many, I'll like to share the two I believe will evoke all others: namely, the role of *prayer* and *submission*.

First of all, please understand that prayer is essential in any godly relationship. It is the link that connects us to God. It is the means by which we talk to Him. You've heard many say, prayer is the key. Let me re-affirm—it is. What is the purpose of a key? Simply put, to unlock. Let prayer unlock whatever needs to be open in your marriage and in you, whether a need for better focus, communication, respecting boundaries, or working through differences. I dare you to put prayer on that need. Philippians 4:6 encourages: "... in everything by prayer and supplication with thanksgiving let your requests be made known to God...". In light of this, I hope you won't be the spouse that regrets, *"I should have spent more time on my knees, instead of saying and doing as I pleased.*

This leads me to the second vital role: submission. Spiritually speaking, submission is the act of accepting or yielding to God's authority above yourselves and all others. But first, do you know that prayer is the role that aids the submission process? It is prayer which makes submission possible. I believe one reason why "will wars" erupts in a marriage is because couples lack a clear understanding of these two specific roles. Over the years, I can't tell you the times my husband and I have bumped heads (in need of spiritual ice-packs) from not respecting these two roles. We've found, knowing and doing what the Bible says on prayer and submission will eliminate a lot of head butting.

We now realize that in our marriage, adhering to God's authority produces submitting to one another. Ephesians 5:21-23 tells us why we should submit, and how we should submit: "submitting to one another out of reverence for Christ. Wives, submit to your own husbands, as to the Lord. For the husband is the head of the wife even as Christ is the head of the church, his body, and is himself its Savior." And again, in Colossians 3:19: "Husbands, love your wives, and do not be harsh with them." James 4:7 adds: "Submit yourselves therefore to God. Resist the devil, and he will flee from you." Truly, we need God's help do this.

Also, be mindful that being prayerful and submissive, won't prevent adversity from raising its ugly head. Definitely, understanding your roles will help in building strength when confronting such opposition. Remember, facing adversity is part of being human, and no one, and no marriage is exempt. IPeter 4:12 records: "Beloved, do not be surprised at the fiery trial when it comes upon you to test you, as though something strange were happening to you" Sometimes strange things can happen in your marriage that have nothing to do with what you or your spouse have said or done. As in life, in order for growth to occur, some things are bound to happen. In other words, don't be so quick to throw in the towel. Stand together in Christ, and give the Holy Spirit a chance to work in both your hearts.

The Need for God

When couples recognize the need for God in their marriage, it won't be difficult to embrace the godliness within the marriage. God, not only provides the physical help that is needed, He also provides the spiritual help by giving strength, patience, power, and endurance. Regardless of what you go through, He brings light, joy, and peace in your marriage. Needless to say, all marriages will have challenges of some kind. But with God, marriage can be a whole lot easier and sweeter, even when experiencing the most trying of times.

Recognizing our need for God has definitely helped us, and He's still helping us to get through some tough spots. Oh yes, in marriage, there will be tough spots. We're aware there may be even tougher spots up the road. According to the Bible, just ask Abraham and Sarah—they had Hagar;

Moses and his wife—they had Pharaoh while dealing with the children of Israel; Noah and his wife—they had the flood; Job and his wife—they had sickness, suffering, and judgmental friends; Jacob and his wife—they had trickery, Laban, Leah, and Esau; Joseph and his wife—they had Egypt and Joseph's siblings. From looking at their marriage experiences, their need for God was evident. Still, today, there are countless others who have had (and having) their share of struggles. Thankfully, by leaning and depending on God's strength, many are still standing.

In short, God already knew (by ourselves) marriage would be an impossible task for us to do effectively, and we would need His help. Yet, there are many marriages that think they're doing "marriage" by themselves, living as if they don't need God. Many appear to be happy and successful in life, family, and business, with no recognition of God in the picture. But I say, isn't that just like God to rain His loving mercy on all? He's so patience in waiting for others to come to the knowledge of Him. I can't help but urge married couples, who are not a part of this sacred and intimate union, to take hold of Christ; accept His salvation, and learn what you are missing in Him. Only through Him is there access to His glorious presence, joy in His Holy Spirit, and peace that surpasses all understanding.

We're grateful, by coming to the knowledge of the need for Christ in our marriage, it is far better than it has ever been, despite the struggles we face. We recognize, it is Christ who gives the victory to stand and withstand in this amazing sacred and intimate journey. The scripture reads in John 15:5b: ". . . for apart from me you can do nothing." In Roman 8:37 we read: ". . . in all these things we are more than conqueror through him who loved us."

I admonish you to let Christ rule in your union, and join in the victory of pursuing a marriage for His glory.

CHAPTER *3*

Helpful Hints on the Sacredness of Marriage

*W*e have learned in our marriage that people are quick to give advice; some have good intentions and some do not. Some advice can be positive and others negative. We are, however, grateful to all advice that have proven to be helpful to our marriage. Still, it pays to know what advice to accept. Certainly, having a spiritual ear can provide ways of distinguishing what is helpful in this godly union. Jesus says in Revelation 3:22: "He who has an ear to hear, let him hear what the Spirit says to the churches." With that said, husbands and wives, you also need to hear what the Spirit is saying to you in your marriage. If the Spirit is not advising you to do this or that, turn it down. We have found, if God's Word doesn't say or support the advice offered, then it is to be rejected.

I ask you, since God is the originator of marriage,

doesn't it make sense to listen to Him? On your job, doesn't it make sense to follow your boss's advice 'for the work' if you're employed by him? If not, your job may be in jeopardy. Surely, doing what God has to say is crucial to the stability and success of your marriage. He can set your marriage on a new path.

When my husband and I became aware God had a say in our marriage, our hearts became convicted that we were living our marriage in a selfish way; something had to change. As we know, God doesn't change and neither does His Word. We needed to change from being married our way to seeking the advice found in His Word. To leave the one out, who joined your marriage together, makes it ineffective in the way it was intended. Please note: *God is too intelligent to "photo bomb" any marriage in order to be in it.* He leaves it up to us to invite Him in or not; to listen to Him or not. Surely, following our own advice for marriage will definitely leave Him out of the picture. Below are some helpful hints which encourage my husband and I to embrace this sacred union through prayer and devotion, communication, disagreements, and trials, as supported by God's Word.

Prayer and Devotion: Husbands and wives, you can eliminate a lot of commotion if you begin and end your day with prayer and devotion.

- Meet with God daily in prayer together and separately.
- Pray for a better attitude today than yesterday.
- Pray to maintain a forgiving heart every day.
- Remember, prayer cultivates the habit of sacredness in your marriage.

- If you want a marriage that God will lead, His Holy Word you both must prayerfully read.
- Pray when you understand your spouse, and pray when you don't.
- When things go wrong, first seek God's help on your knees; not on the phone.

"Continue steadfastly in prayer, being watchful in it with thanksgiving" (Colossians 4:2).

"Therefore, confess your sins to one another and pray for one another, that ye may be healed. The prayer of a righteous person has great power as it is working" (James 5:16).

Communication: *Husbands and wives, there's nothing wrong in speaking with your spouse in a loving and godly tone.*

- Fill your hearts with the Word of God.
- Welcome silence when it comes to individually commune with God.
- Be careful how you use words; they carry weight and power.
- Don't hold your heart hostage with unspoken words; decide intentionally to communicate.
- If you want your voice to be heard, communicate with pleasant words; this brings the damper down to the right sound.
- Wait to be heard.

"Let no corrupting talk come out of your mouths, but only such as is good for building up, as fits the occasion, that it may give grace to those who hear" (Ephesians 4:29).

"Gracious words are like a honeycomb, sweetness to the soul and health to the body." (Proverbs 16:24)

Disagreements: *Husbands and wives, there will be times in your marriage when you may get really heated; here are some helpful hints I believe are really needed.*

- With all might seek God's advice, even when you're feeling a little up-tight.
- Refusing to stress about the small stuff can eliminate a lot of fuss.
- Talk over issues in the privacy of your home; this way, you won't go wrong.
- Don't let your disagreements snowball into arguments.
- When you disagree, discuss; seek God's help before things get rough.
- Never attempt to stunt your spouse's growth by stomping on their thoughts.
- Settle disagreements before settling down for the night; you'll sleep much better.

"Remind them of these things, and charge them before God not to quarrel about words, which does no good, but only ruins the hearers" (2 Timothy 2:14).
"Do all things without grumbling or disputing," (Philippians 2:14).

Trials: *Husbands and wives, a Christian marriage doesn't exempt you from the trials of life, but you can get through them better by holding on to Christ.*

- In marriage, there will always be tests.
- When trials come, don't let your first reaction be to run; go to God in prayer.

- Keep standing on your faith; not on your feelings, or your spouse's faults.
- Trust God in the trials; only through Him you can triumph.
- Remember, you are not immune from the trials of life; so... stop crying.
- Trials are not trails we make, but tests we take.
- There's a purpose in the trial; trust God, and keep holding on.

"Count it all joy, my brothers, when you meet trials of various kinds, for you know that the testing of your faith produces steadfastness. And let steadfastness have its full effect, that you may be perfect and complete, lacking in nothing" (James 1:2-4).

"Blessed is the man who remains steadfast under trial, for when he has stood the test he will receive the crown of life, which God has promised to those who love him" (James 1:12).

CHAPTER 4

Embracing the Intimacy of Marriage

*I*ntimacy, (in its genuine form) stems from God. It is that close connection which makes one *know* that they are loved, belonged, wanted, valued, needed, appreciated, and so very special. Who doesn't want this kind of intimacy demonstrated in their union? It can be embraced from the beginning and throughout. Husbands and wives, do you know marriage and intimacy are not mutually exclusive? They can go together as easily and tastefully as peanut butter and jelly—spreading better and easier over time, as you merge together in Christ. As you grow in love, grow in intimacy.

Think about it, what would marriage be like without the intimacy of your spouse's embrace, time, attention, participation, or care? On a higher and greater level, what would God be like if He had no intimacy? What would worship be if we couldn't feel or experience His loving embrace? Those who know the love of God, know this is unimaginable and unfathomable! Our God is ever-present with arms wide open to embrace His children in a loving and gracious way. God is love, and His love is what He so willingly gives to whosoever. John reminds us: "We love because he first loved us" (1 John 4:19). God was the first to embrace with His love.

Are you aware, embracing God (The Intimate One), can help you demonstrate your affection for each other in ways you may have never known? Have you considered allowing Him to live in the midst of your marriage could make intimacy seem as good as floating on a cloud (so to speak)? Intimacy could even be as wonderful as observing all the soft pillows in your home, finding none so comfortable as the one you lay your head in your own bedroom.

In marriage, you will discover, true intimacy is not just one thing, or one-sided; it's a packaged deal. It's spiritual, physical, sexual, emotional, social, domestic, communicative, interactive, supportive, and financial— to say the least. All these contribute to the marriage's nourishing process. One without the other can be a matter of concern and may put a chill on the life-long honeymoon. I hope you will realize, by including your spouse in all areas of intimacy will be a good way to embrace and build your union in a loving and God-glorifying way.

For those of you who feel true intimacy is lacking in your marriage, in one or more of these areas, first know that intimacy begins with you. Start by being loving and understanding. *Communicate* and *socialize* with your spouse as much as possible. Be *interactive* and not passive; be present in the moment. Merge together in worship and pray to connect *spiritually, physically, emotionally, domestically* and *sexually.* Don't forget to *support* one another in your dreams and goals, and always stay on the same page in *financial* matters and concerns. In brief, put your best foot forward to let your spouse know that you value and respect them in every realm of intimacy.

Also, be intentional to add *fun* in your intimacy package. Make it a habit to fill it with love and laughter. In addition to this, also include the FUN of *Faithfulness, Unity,* and *Nurturing.* As you will soon see, the sum of these three can really spike up your intimacy levels in building trust, promoting oneness, and fostering tenderness. Please strive not to let your marriage be over and done for the lack of FUN. Other than the house of the Lord, I hope engaging in this kind of FUN will make your marriage one of the happiest places on earth you'd rather be!

One spouse, from a seasoned godly married union, once shared with me: *"To live in a marriage without intimacy and fun is like living and sleeping with a rock— and that's mighty hard. If you didn't begin that way, you don't have to end that way. Your intimacy doesn't have to dwindle, diminish, deteriorate, or die. You can fight for your intimacy."* Now since we're all lacking in some areas, let us ask God to show us ways to embrace the intimacy of our marriage, so that it will flourish and grow in the way it should. Be confident, God will show you if you're willing to be shown.

I ask again, have you thought what your marriage would *really* be like without the intimacy of your spouse' embrace? Unfortunately, some couples do know. For others, it's hard to imagine not be able to experience that closeness, that bond, that binds two hearts together as one in Christ. Husbands and wives, I implore you, don't be found guilty of denying your spouse the kind of intimacy they deserve from you. Now here's the question: How to attain and maintain such intimacy throughout a union? As my husband and I have come to know, before intimacy can be what it's meant to be in a marriage, there are a few things to be considered.

Interested in Intimacy?

Wouldn't you admit, before intimacy can be embraced, there must be an interest in it? Is it possible to lovingly embrace anyone that you're not interested in? Certainly not. Sadly to say, when a physical relationship has lost its interest, it usually dies. It dies in every realm of intimacy; the close ties have been severed. That's unfortunate, however, since we know our God is a promoter of marriage, love, and intimacy.

First of all, be assured that God *is* interested in the intimacy of/with His children. He wants to be intimate with you. Just as you love to be consulted, talked to, cherished, and embraced, so does the Lord. So, if you desire to be intimate with God, sacrifice some alone time with Him; demonstrate how much you value the closeness that you share through worship, prayer, and praise; and let Him be your *first* to be acknowledged in the morning, and your *last* to embraced at night.

Secondly, God is also concerned about your marriage as it relates to intimacy. He is the Marriage Counselor and Advisor. He's there to guide it in every realm. He appreciates you coming together in His presence, bringing all your marital hopes and concerns to Him. If you need a listening ear, He'll willingly be your therapist, free of charge. Lie on His spiritual couch, and let Him show you how to work through everything. Though He already knows, don't leave anything out; He's paying attention and is personally there for each of you—your marriage is no exception.

I ask you, are you interested in having an endearing relationship with your spouse that will stand the test of time? More so, are you interested in being intimate with God that will stand the test for eternity? If you are, you're on your way to building a powerful marriage that glorifies God. Continue adoring Him, and watch how close your relationship grows in Him and with each other. My husband and I are learning, *letting God be our bosom buddy is showing us how to stay lovey dovey.*

Lastly, if you are interested in true intimacy (I can't say it enough), seek God in His Word. In it you will find Him demonstrating His love for all people. In John 14:23: "Jesus answered him, 'If anyone loves me, he will keep my word, and my Father will love him, and we will come to him and make our home with him.' " Now how intimate is that!!! Let's be thankful our God is interested in us in such a way to live "in us"—if we love Him. To "live in" is about as close as one can get, wouldn't you say? *Husbands and wives, don't be found guilty of intimate neglect with God or each other.* Know that our interest in God will always be a welcome embrace, which He will never turn away.

Don't Be Unequally Yoked

For intimacy to take place effectively, it's also important for spouses to be on the same page in their faith. For those anticipating marriage, Jesus laid a great foundation in providing the prerequisite for this most sacred and intimate union. To intimately embrace it, His requirement is a must. The Bible said in 2 Corinthians 6:14: "Do not be

unequally yoked with unbelievers. For what partnership
has righteousness with lawlessness? Or what fellowship
has light with darkness?" In other words, God's design is
that believers should be married to believers; both must
be born again. This is not a suggestion; it's God's plan for
marriage.

My husband (being the outdoorsman, that he is) once
said, "Even though God loves all His creation, you will
never find eagles soaring with crows, or sheep grazing
with wolves." His point being, an unbeliever and a believer
cannot soar together productively except they are grazing
from the same pasture of faith. If there's no oneness of
faith, there will be a great divide. I encourage you, if you
desire a marriage pleasing to God, equip yourselves with
the same mind and spirit in the faith of the Lord Jesus
Christ.

You may have heard people say: "Like minds think
alike"; "Association begets assimilation"; "Birds of a feather
flock together." For common statements like these to be
repeated over the years, there must be some validity, if
only through observation and experience. Amos 3:3 (KJV)
asks the question: "Can two walk together except they be
agreed?" Of course, the answer is "no." In other words, to
walk together, the two must have come to an agreement to
meet, talk, pray, live, etc., or there'll be no meeting in mind
or purpose. Spiritually speaking, husbands and wives, two
cannot walk together effectively "as one" if they are not
in accord that Jesus is Lord.

Nevertheless, if you are already married to an
unbeliever, the Bible has an encouraging word for you.
There is hope for your marriage and the unbelieving
spouse. If your unbelieving spouse is willing to stay with
you, then stay. I Corinthians 7:13-14a states: "If any woman
has a husband who is an unbeliever, and he consents

to live with her, she should not divorce him. For the unbelieving husband is made holy because of his wife, and the unbelieving wife is made holy because of her husband." Also, verse 16 encourages: "For how do you know, wife, whether you will save your husband? Or, how do you know husband, whether you will save your wife? So, *husbands and wives, don't miss out, I hope you realize that God's marriage plan is the best plan for you and your spouse.*

I Need You; You Need Me

As we know, intimacy is a basic human need; it is important. It's definitely paramount to fully embrace this marriage union. In the simplest terms, intimacy, according to the Webster's New Dictionary, means to be closely acquainted, or familiar. Husbands and wives, make it your aim to get closely acquainted with your spouse so that your intimacy will deepen. Get to know your spouse on the inside. Learn their wants, needs, hopes, dreams, vision for themselves, your union, and ultimately their vision for God.

When we think of need, we think of that which is necessary, important, a must. Hopefully, as you become aware of the need and purpose of God in your marriage, intimacy with your spouse won't be hard to find. Intimacy dialogue says and knows: "I need you, you need me, and we both need God." You need Him to show you each other's needs, and how to best meet them. Your spouse doesn't simply *want* to be intimate with you, your spouse needs to be intimate with you. As previously mentioned, your spouse needs to feel connected in every realm of your union. As many have experienced, *only "saying" the I do doesn't result in intimacy—"doing" the I do does.*

Husbands and wives, don't be afraid to tell your spouse what you need in your marriage, not so much of what you want. We are aware that love and respect are two of the most profound needs in a marriage, a love and respect for God—and each other. God's Word affirms in Ephesians 5:33: "However, let each one of you love his wife as himself, and let the wife see that she respects her husband." Inclusive of these, there are other needs to be met. You may be surprise at how easily recognizable they are.

Consider for a moment: In the physical realm, a new born babe needs everything from its parents. It needs to be loved, fed, held, embraced, nurtured, clothed, and sheltered. Without these needs being met, the baby will not survive in a healthy way, or not at all. Husbands and wives, consider your marriage as needing most things a new born baby will need, and ask God to help you do them for your spouse. If you want your marriage to survive and flourish, love your spouse (with God's love); feed your spouse (physically, emotionally, and spiritually); hold your spouse (dearly and sincerely); embrace and nurture your spouse (closely and *often*). Be mindful, anything that is done often will be remembered and might easily be reciprocated. Let your spouse know how much he/she means to you—*often!*

Imitate God's Intimate Love

Husbands and wives, if you want your intimacy to be all it can be, strive to imitate God's intimate love in your marriage. If you both are being led by the Spirit of God, then you know that it is the Spirit who provides revelation on how to pattern after His love. It is He that makes you aware, to imitate God's intimate love calls for being loving, sacrifice, humility, forgiveness, and gratitude. Without these, it would be impossible to portray His love. Now let us see how we can best model after them.

First, to imitate God's intimate love is to be loving. It is to live in and walk in God's love. As we have seen, real intimacy is manifested from the love of God. Being intimate with Him helps us appreciate the love we share with our spouses. Even when we don't feel like loving, loving is still God's way and reflects our deep passion for Him. Therefore, we should aim to live in our marriages in a way that our spouses have no doubt that we love them, but our first and endless love is God. Jesus says in Matthew 22:37: "...You shall love the LORD your God with all your heart, and with all your soul and with all your mind." By letting God be your *first* and *most* loved, there shouldn't be a problem loving your spouse God's way.

Secondly, to imitate God's intimate love calls for sacrifice. "Then Jesus told his disciples, 'if anyone would come after me, let him deny himself and take up his cross and follow me' " (Matthew 16:24). Yes, walking in God's love will cause us to give up something we may not want—*self*; our ego. Many times, we don't won't to let go of self because it hurts our pride. But what pride has to do with it? Nothing. Pride is everything that is not of God. It hinders from living in love God's way. Remember, love doesn't kick up dust or stir up a fuss; being prideful does. Love has a way of clearing the air; being prideful suffocates. Now that the air is cleared, we understand that walking in pride "clearly" is not imitating God's love. So, how should we walk?

Thirdly, we should walk in humility. Humility is the way of Christ. James 4:10 encourages: "Humble yourselves before the Lord, and he will lift you up." Husbands and wives, practice being humble toward one another. Again, even when you may not feel like being humble. I encourage you to choose humility anyway for the sake of peace, your marriage, and for the love of Christ. I say to you, *isn't it far time to start walking in humility, and stop battling for right-ness?* If there is no humility, there'll be no *right-ness* for you, nor *right-ness* for your spouse. Humility says and knows, "It's the righteousness and right-ness of Christ that matters." Once you can agree on that, you are ready to imitate God's intimate love in humility.

Another way to imitate God's intimate love is by forgiving. Again, when times arise that you don't feel like forgiving, acknowledge, "I forgive." Then, trust God to do the work in your heart. Why? Because forgiving is also the way of Christ. He's not a God that holds grudges. He forgave and He wants us to do the same. Ephesians 4:32 admonishes: "Be kind to one another, tenderhearted, forgiving one another, as God in Christ forgave you." Remember, prayer is the key, and it's available to request God's help in restoring forgiveness back in your heart.

Last, but not least, to imitate God's intimate love is to possess the spirit of gratitude. We are encouraged in I Chronicles 16:34: "Oh give thanks to the Lord, for he is good; for his steadfast love endures forever!" Knowing this should cause you to walk in gratitude for God and for each other. Be thankful that it is His grace which provides the strength and power to exemplify the kind of love that keeps on loving in spite of. Also, be thankful that God has chosen you out of all the people in the world to be in *your* marriage. God knew what He was doing when you first laid eyes on each other. He also knew the challenges that would inevitably come and grow you both into His purpose.

Today, if you've been lacking in expressing the love of God towards your spouse, let this be a great time to start. Ask God to help you demonstrate the kind of love that glorifies Him in being loving, with humility, sacrifice, forgiveness, and gratitude. Then keep on thanking Him for the awareness that embracing His love is strong enough to keep you both loving. We're also reminded in Ephesians 5:1-2: "Therefore be imitators of God, as beloved children. And walk in love, as Christ loved us and gave himself up for us, a fragrant offering and sacrifice to God."

Embrace God's Intimate Union

Another way to embrace the intimacy in your marriage is by embracing God's intimate union. This is one of the Father, Son, and Holy Spirit. They are one and work together as one. To embrace the Father is to embrace the Son. To embrace the Son is to embrace the Holy Spirit, and vice versa. Colossians 2:9-10 lets us know: "For in him the whole fullness of deity dwells bodily, and you have been filled in him, who is the head of all rule and authority." So, as you and your spouse are one in your union, it pays to recognize this most holy and sacred one.

Being united with this union provides power that will help your marriage be all it can be to the glory of God. Grab hold to it, as if hanging on for dear life. Why? Because this union is a *life force*; a life sustaining force that will produce life and add life within your marriage. Jesus said in John 10:10: "The thief comes only to steal and kill and destroy. I came that they may have life and have it abundantly." Sadly to say, a marriage that is not joined together in Christ is lacking this life-force and is a spiritually dead union. My husband and I believe that trying to embrace intimacy without embracing God's intimate union can leave us lifeless, loveless, and wanting in so many ways.

Know that God is one God, and it is He that helps us to live as one in our marriage. Jesus also declares in John 10:30: "I and the Father are one." If we fail to embrace Him, we fail to realize and appreciate the suffering that God did for us through Him. Jesus died that we might come alive and be united in God. He paid the price of sin so that we would be partakers *with Him* in glory. He rose in victory defeating sin's hold, thereby allowing freedom and access to embrace the Father. Right now, you and your spouse also have the privilege to cling to and look to the Father, Son, and Holy Spirit within your marriage.

Just as there is no way we can embrace our union without being married, there is no way we can embrace God's intimate union without being married to Him in love, faith, and obedience. Yes, I am aware man have left the word "obey" out of some marriage vows—but God hasn't. With Christ, obedience is utmost. It is obedience to Him, in love and faith, that builds the relationship in this holy union. For we, the church, is the Bride of Christ, and He is our Bridegroom. Being united in Him produces a closeness, a bond that extends beyond time into eternity. The Bible speaks of this closeness in Romans 8:35: "Who shall separate us from the love of Christ? Shall tribulation, or distress or persecution, or famine, or nakedness, or danger, or sword?" Verse 38–39 affirms: "For I am sure that neither death nor life, nor angels nor rulers, nor things present nor things to come, nor powers, nor height nor depth, nor anything else in all creation will be able to separate us from the love of God in Christ Jesus our Lord."

The Bible also promises that everyone who has accepted Jesus as Savior are included in this holy life-giving union.

It includes those who have been born by the Spirit of God, and called by His name out from darkness into His marvelous light. 2 Corinthians 4:8-9 also tells of those "... afflicted in every way, but not crushed; perplexed, but not driven to despair; persecuted, but not forsaken; struck down, but not destroyed; always carrying in the body the death of Jesus, so that the life of Jesus may also be manifested in our bodies." As a result, making it possible not only to be united with Christ in this world, but also in the world to come.

It is in the book of Revelation that informs us of this great event, with the assurance that embracing God's intimate union doesn't end in this world, but will transcend to the hereafter. John, while on the Isle of Patmos, gives us a future look at this intimate union we will share in Christ: "Then I heard what seemed to be the voice of a great multitude, like the roar of many waters and like the sound of mighty peals of thunder, crying out, "Hallelujah! For the Lord our God the Almighty reigns. Let us rejoice and exult and give him the glory, for the marriage of the Lamb has come, and his Bride has made herself ready; it was granted her to clothe herself with fine linen, bright and pure" for the fine linen is the righteous deeds of the saints" (Revelation 19:6-8).

Ah! What a wonderful vision of the eternity of this union with Christ and His Bride! So be encouraged, husbands and wives, although our physical marriages will end in time, let's be grateful the marriage of the Bride and the Lamb will never end. It will last forever; no fall outs, separation, break-ups, or divorce. As we grow in grace and in the knowledge of the Lord and Savior Jesus Christ, let's embrace the union we have with Him now, as we're looking forward to a greater celebration of one to come!

CHAPTER 5

Helpful Hints on the Intimacy of Marriage

ould you agree, we all could use a little help or advice (every now and then) in the way of intimacy? Help in finding ways to gain that special closeness that will sweep us off our feet? It's not surprising to see headlines on newspaper articles, magazine covers, book titles, reality shows, or pop ups from the internet on sharing advice on how to make your mate happy. How to spruce up your intimacy? Or, how to have the best marriage ever? Some goes on to share what to do next, if what's being done isn't working. If we're honest, we may have tried some of this advice... and still didn't find what we were hoping for.

Sometimes, however, when we follow a well of advice, we can come up short. This may happen because every relationship is unique and requires special handling. Being aware that there is so much advice on relationship issues, I hope you don't let your union suffer by searching in the wrong places. Looking in the wrong places could leave a couple confused, not knowing what will work and what won't. I submit to you, why not try God's advice? He promises in Proverbs 32:8: "I will instruct you and teach you in the way you should go; I will counsel you with my eye upon you." Truly, God will gladly guide us in our marriages if we ask Him. He will let us know what will work in search for true intimacy.

Simply by searching the scriptures, we can discover how to recognize true intimacy, and what it takes to maintain it in the marriage. They can certainly provide the best information on developing an intimate relationship that no literature or social media can possibly match. I urge you to read what God has to say. You will soon realize He has the best Word on any subject, especially on the subject of love and respect. Understanding that there can be no intimacy without these two, I would like to share some helpful hints that have made it easier for my husband and I to embrace love and respect in our marriage, as supported by God's Word.

Helpful Hints on Love

Love for God

Husbands and wives, let there be no doubt, walking in God's love is the best way for you and your spouse.

- Above all, love and embrace God with all you've got; He is the Lover.
- Let your love for God be your strongest motivation in anything.

- God didn't fall in love with you; He's always loved you!
- Loving God's way isn't selfish, and it will never go unrewarded.
- The only love potion you'll ever need is God; O taste and see!
- God's way of love is never too much, will never run out, but will overflow.
- Raise your love for God; He's already risen for you!

"As the Father has loved me, so have I loved you. Abide in my love" (John 15:9).

"Keep yourselves in the love of God, waiting for the mercy of our Lord Jesus Christ that leads to eternal life" (Jude v-21).

Love for Spouse

Husbands and wives, let your spouse know that they are loved: L—loved every day; O—okay in every way; V- vital to your union; and E—enough, that there be no need for anyone else.

- Love your spouse with humility, not hostility.
- Since love can be resurrected, so can the honeymoon.
- Loving right can stimulate the appetite.
- Distance does not make the heart grow fonder— love does.
- Initiate, cultivate, and illustrate love to your spouse; it'll grow better.
- Come what may, use love's power to overcome it.
- Be a lovely spouse, in attitude, aptitude, fortitude, and gratitude.

"Wives, submit to your own husbands as is fitting in the Lord. Husbands, love your wives, and do not be harsh with them" (Colossians 3:18-19).

"Let all that you do be done in love" (1Corinthians 16:14).

Helpful Hints for Husbands on Love

- Cherish your wife for the sake of Christ; by this God is glorified in your life.
- After Christ, your next love and priority is your wife.
- Exemplify love for your wife at home and anywhere you roam.
- Activate love for your wife with gentleness and not grumpiness.
- Demonstrate love for your wife in word and in action.

"Husbands, love your wives, as Christ loved the church and gave himself up for her, that he might sanctify her, having cleansed her by the washing of water with the word," (Ephesians 5:25-26).

"In the same way husbands should love their wives as their own bodies, He who loves his wife loves himself' (Ephesians 5:28).

A Love Poem for Husbands

Since one of the primary needs of a wife is to be loved,
here's a poem that reminds my husband,
I am his given from above.

Husbands, love your wives. God
wants you to enjoy her,
Adore her, pray for her, and also
play with her; she does too.
Yes, play with her. Date her. This
may sound a bit corny,
But sometimes sing sweet songs of melody in her ear.
Whisper and say loving words to her every day.
Don't treat her as a mother figure or an employee
To only work and clean for you.
Remember, she was your bride,
That captured you with her loving and gentle eyes.
Now she has blossomed to be your beautiful wife,
Given to you by the Lord Jesus Christ.
You've heard the song... "Treat Her Like A Lady";
Not only that... treat her like your loving "Baby,"
So that she'll feel your loving embrace
Way after you leave for the work day.

Helpful Hints for Wives on Love

- Wives, the lovely way is to love God's way.
- Be kindly affectionate to your husband.
- Love your God-given man; all others... ban.
- After Christ, your husband is the next love in your life.
- Don't wear your love like an accessory; never take it off.

"And so train the young women to love their husbands and children." Titus 2:4

An excellent wife who can find? She is far more precious than jewels. The heart of her husband trusts in her, and he will have no lack of gain. She does him good, and not harm, all the days of her life" (Prov 31:10-11).

Helpful Hints on Respect

Respect for God

Husbands and wives, God deserves your utmost respect.

- Respect God above all.
- If you respect God, respecting your spouse shouldn't be hard.
- Respect what God says about marriage, His plan and design.
- Base your marriage on godly principles, not earthly practices or worldly values.
- Follow God's example on respect.
- God is not concerned about your loyalty when you respect His authority.

"But in your hearts honor Christ the Lord as holy, always being prepared to make a defense to anyone who asks you for the reason for the hope that is in you; yet do it with gentleness and respect," (1 Peter 3:15).

"Let every person be subject to the governing authorities. For there is no authority except from God, and those that exist have been instituted by God" (Roman 13:1).

Respect for Spouse

Husbands and wives, you will regret if you fail the test of respect.

- Disrespecting your spouse isn't respectful.
- Respect who your spouse is in the marriage, God does.
- Respect your spouse's voice and choice.
- When you dress, wear respect.
- Respecting ears listen; respecting mouths wait its turn.
- Your spouse deserves and expects respect.

Love one another with brotherly affection. Outdo one another in showing honor" (Romans 12:10).

"Let marriage be held in honor among all, and let the marriage bed be undefiled, for God will judge the sexually immoral and adulterous" (Hebrews 13:4).

Helpful Hints for Husbands on Respect

- When you wake and see your wife, always say something nice.
- Husbands, do not attempt to school, fool, or rule your wife; it just doesn't work.
- Remember you are not your own; you belong to God and so does your wife.
- Besides Christ, let your wife know she matters most in the marriage.
- Always be a husband at home, and when you travel alone.

"Likewise, husbands, live with your wives in an

understanding way, showing honor to the woman as the weaker vessel, since they are heirs with you of the grace of life, so that your prayers may not be hindered" (1 Peter 3:7).

"Show yourself in all respects to be a model of good works, and in your teaching show integrity, dignity, and sound speech that cannot be condemned, so that an opponent may be put to shame, having nothing evil to say about us" (Titus 2:7-8).

Helpful Hints for Wives on Respect

- Wives, give your husband your best respect.
- Respect the man of the house—as the man of the house.
- When you first see your husband hug him; don't bug him.
- Remember your husband is designed to be God's leader in the home; respect God's leadership.
- Respecting your husband is never a bad thing; it's all good.
- Respect your husband as "the man," and respect God as "God"; don't get confused.

"Likewise, wives, be subject to your own husbands, so that even if some do not obey the word, they may be won without a word by the conduct of their wives, when they see your respectful and pure conduct." (1 Peter 3:1).

"She does him good, and not harm, all the days of her life" (Proverbs 31:12).

A Respectful Poem for Wives

Since one of the primary needs of husbands is respect,

I'll like to share a poem that helps
me remember just that.
Wives, respect your husbands.
Love him.
He is your man of all the men in this great land.
God prepared him for you.
He knew your husband would bring out of you
What was missing in him and vice versa.
God has given you both what you need,
In order to make your marriage work, indeed.
Wives, listen to your husbands.
I can't express it enough… listen to "your" husband.
Always lend him a receptive ear.
If you doubt his advice,
You can ask the Lord and Savior Jesus Christ.
Tell Him your concern,
And don't worry about the rest;
For God has a way of granting every request.
So, wives, it's best to treat your husband like a "man"
And not like a "boy,"
Even though he is your only God-given "play toy."
Buy him a rattle sometimes!
Shake it to him;
He just might fall in line.

Helpful Hints on Appreciation, Pride, and Leadership

In addition to love and respect, here are a few more
helpful hints for husbands and wives that have
proven to be an encouragement to us in embracing

the intimacy in our marriage on *appreciation, pride, and leadership,* as supported by God's Word

Appreciation

Husbands and wives, one way to make your spouse's heart to smile is to say, "thank you"; saying it often, it shouldn't be hard to do.

- Live in your marriage with a grateful heart.
- Be thankful for a godly companion; you need no further to look for another.
- Be thankful you always have someone to consult in your marriage—God.
- Appreciate the moments with your spouse; make the most of them.
- Indeed, be thankful for the care you receive.
- Saying "thank you" can never be wasted; say it anyhow and often.
- Celebrate and surprise your spouse sometimes—just because.

"And let the peace of God rule in your hearts, to which indeed you were called in one body. And be thankful." Colossians 3:15

"And whatever you do, in word or deed, do everything in the name of the Lord Jesus, giving thanks to God the Father through him." Colossians 3:17

Husbands, above all:

- Be thankful God has given you a helpmeet; don't her value deplete or delete.

- Be thankful for the opportunity to be a husband; you were chosen, no one else.
- Your wife will appreciate more loving, listening, and less lecturing.

Wives, above all:

- Let your husband know you are his number one fan.
- Show your husband you hear and appreciate what he says.
- Eliminate the nagging, and on your husband start bragging.

"Let there be no filthiness nor foolish talk nor crude joking, which are out of place, but instead let there be thanksgiving" (Ephesians 5:4).

Pride

Husbands and wives, don't let pride be the actor nor spokesperson in your marriage.

- Combat pridefulness with prayerfulness.
- Setting aside pride helps keep your marriage on the rise—in humility.
- It's humbling to admit when your spouse is really right; ask God for strength.
- Pride hinders the relationship with your spouse by leaving you on the outs.
- Eventually, pride will strip you and skin you in the worst way.
- Beware, pride is a loaded gun that doesn't need a trigger.

- Pride and sin have one thing in the center: "I"; don't let that be you.
- Live in unity with your spouse; don't let pride disarm the harmony in your house.

"When pride comes, then comes disgrace, but with the humble is wisdom" (Proverbs 11:2).

"With all humility and gentleness, with patience, bearing with one another in love, eager to maintain the unity of the Spirit in the bond of peace" (Ephesians 4:2-3).

Leadership

Husbands:

- It's better to lead than to push, insist, force, or demand.
- Husbands, follow God's Word, no matter what you've heard.
- Lead your home with prayer, love, respect, and devotion.
- Lead with the awareness that you are following the leader—God.
- God is the marriage planner and designer, not you; follow His blueprint.
- God's road map on marriage is found in the Holy Bible; use its trail.
- Remember, leading and serving goes hand in hand.

"But not so with you. Rather, let the greatest among you become as the youngest, and the leader as one who serves" (Luke 22:26).

"Be watchful, stand firm in the faith, act like men, be strong" (1Corinthians 16:13).

Wives:

- Remember, God said it: "the husband is the head of the wife."
- Never attempt to lead your husband; pray for him and his decisions.
- Pray for God's guidance for you both.
- If your husband is following God, following him shouldn't be hard.
- Pray for your husbands; if change is needed, God knows how.
- Helping your husband's leadership to be a success, you both will win!
- Wives, remembering God's order will keep you in the right step.

"For the husband is the head of the wife even as Christ is head of the church, his body, and is himself its Savior" Ephesians 5:23).

"But I want you to understand that the head of every man is Christ, the head of a wife is her husband, and the head of Christ is God" (I Corinthians 11:3).

Enhancing Romance

*A*t this point, you've read many helpful hints on embracing the intimacy of marriage. By now, you may have added a few of your own. Still, there is one more I'd like to share: don't forget about romance; it's important too. Embrace it. Enrich it. Make it your own. Let romance be one of the priorities that make up your happy home. My husband and I are endeavoring to *keep the romance flowing so that a lot of nonsense will be going away.*

I understand that romance, or being romantic is a relative term. It can mean and apply different things for different people. When I speak of being romantic in terms of intimacy, I'm referring to that which is characterized by genuine love: loving deeply, tenderly, and passionately; not with feelings only, but with action. Husbands and wives, romance calls for action! I also understand, however, that at the onset of any relationship, especially in the early years of marriage, feelings can be monumental. You may remember at the beginning how you and your spouse were so romantic, "woo-hooing" and "goo-gooing" in each other's eyes as if no one mattered in the world but you two. Just being wrapped up in that initial feeling was romantic enough. Can you relate? I bet you can!

Definitely, this can be a very exciting and explorative transition for you both. Initially, you think you will wake up with butterflies and heart fluttering every day! But eventually, real life happens. What then? What are you going to do when the spontaneity of the heart fluttering ceases, and the butterflies seem to take a flight? Well, let me encourage you—you can enhance your romance. Don't push the panic button; push the romantic button. Start finding strategic ways to cultivate and create that heart fluttering and butterfly effect. If you still love each other, those feelings can be resurrected. They are not dead; they only need to be revived. I urge you, please don't give up on those *feel-ly* feelings of excitement in your union. If the thrill appears to be winding down, there are ways you can make a comeback (if you want to 'come' back)!

I remember a time when my husband attempted to put his best foot forward in sprucing up the romance department. We had been married for some years now and much of our time was focused on raising our four lovely children; not much time for romance, I assure you. It happened that on one anniversary, he bought me a stuffed animal of an American eagle wearing a tall red, white, and blue top hat with one of its fingers pointing out! Being a Vietnam veteran, and knowing his admiration for eagles, I could clearly see him buying a gift like that for himself. But for me? Oh no, not on such a special occasion! Although I admire his patriotism, yet to present me with an American eagle for our anniversary, I thought all the butterflies had suddenly flown away and died! At first, I was nearly in tears seeing that patriot eagle with its one huge finger seemingly extending out at me on my anniversary! I was literally undone. "How could he dare think this was romantic!" Then at the base of the stuffed statue-type figure I saw the caption, which read in big bold red, white, and blue letters: "I WANT YOU!" Oh ... wow ... my heart melted! And yes, we made a comeback! Enough said.

Let me encourage you, since God knows about love and intimacy, I'm certain He knows about those feelings of romance, and the joy it can bring to a couple. He understands what the "heart fluttering" and "tummy butterflies" are all about in this sacred and intimate union. Even though God is a Spirit, He's still aware of "all" human feelings and emotions, and He knows spouses appreciate being romanced by one another. I don't think we would be out of order to solicit His advice in hopes of bringing a little added spice, excitement, and wonderment to this beautiful relationship. I say to my husband sometimes... "To love and be loved is exceptional! To be intimate is great! But to be romantic is delightful!"

Besides the feeling of excitement, however, when a couple make up their minds to get married, they may encounter an array of other emotions; nervousness, wondering, anxiety, worrying, and even doubting. Still, when one decides to tie the knot, i.e., they may have felt at least two or more of these feelings. But don't worry; it's natural. Experiencing such feelings don't necessarily mean you should back out of your impending commitment. Being that it is a huge step of faith, simply keep seeking God's guidance.

Actually, there is no way a new couple can see the gravity, or true reality of this commitment. It could be similar to purchasing a new vehicle for the first time.

Initially, you admire it every day just for the beauty of it. It doesn't have to do anything but let you ride smoothly. But don't drive it a few times just to discover a scratch or dent on it. Oh boy, that can be very disturbing if you're looking "only" at the outside. You may have thought, "How did my beautiful vehicle get scratched? Where did that dent come from? I parked it in a safe place. Yet, it got damaged!" I tell you (if you're like many of us), after you've had the vehicle a while, you won't be so sensitive to notice every nick, scratch or dent. Instead, you become grateful that your vehicle is still running!

Thanks be to God, many of us don't get rid of our vehicle! We keep it. Why? Because in spite of those imperfections, we begin to see the vehicle for what it truly is… a good, reliable, and trustworthy mode of traveling. If you're of sound mind, body, and spirit, you'll want to keep the maintenance on the vehicle you chose. One way of doing this is by enhancing it on the inside as well as on the outside. Hopefully then, you will get and maintain the ride of your life!

With that scenario, I hope I didn't put a small damper on marriage. My point being, on this sacred and intimate journey, you and your spouse are going to experience many changes within your union. But the good news is, if you both maintain an active prayer life, devote yourselves to God and each other, you won't see a need to get rid of *the vehicle of your marriage*. You can keep driving, even though the road may get rocky sometimes. What am I saying? There is something you can do to fine-tune the vehicle of your marriage that will keep it looking, sounding, and performing like new.

You can enhance your romance by keeping the line of communication open; by letting your words be adoring and inviting. If you're holding on to grudges, let them go;

for holding grudges can definitely hinder the romantic water from flowing. Be the first to forgive, and most importantly, keep loving affectionally by demonstrating the kind of love you want in return. I John 3:18 says: "Little children, let us not love in word or talk but in deed and in truth." Sometimes, husbands and wives, we can literally talk too much. In the romance department, actions do speak louder than words! Remember, just looking at candy or flowers in a store don't move them off the shelf.

There is more good news. For those who have been married a significant amount of years, please note, romance doesn't have to end when your marriage extends. The late honorable Billy Graham sheds light on this word romance. He shared that *"The word 'romance', according to the dictionary, means excitement, adventure, and something extremely real. Romance should last a lifetime."* In other words, I believe Pastor Graham was encouraging spouses that romance should continue as long as their union does: "Until death do you part." Certainly, loving each other God's way can help keep the romance alive, whether you're new to marriage or been married for a while.

Notwithstanding, for a couple to be married a significant amount of years, I wouldn't be surprised if some might wonder if their romance is still alive? Are the flames that were burning at first still holding that blaze? I wish I could say "Yes, it definitely will." But in reality, it depends on the kind of marriage you both desire and are willing to work towards. If, however, the answer is "No," I pray, *Sacred and Intimate Lives of Husbands and Wives* will encourage you both to throw a little more kindling on the fire. God can and is willing to help you revive and maintain that blaze. *(You do know our God is a consuming fire, and He knows how to light a match!).*

Being mindful of those kinds of questions, I pray your

answer is "Yes, we're still romantic; the fire is still burning and has never ceased!" Also, I pray you will add: "Because of the love we share in Christ and for each other, we are confident the romantic flames of holy matrimony will never stop burning as long as we both are …

R   relying on God's guidance in our marriage;
O   observing God's plan for our marriage;
M   mastering our wills by submitting them to God's will;
A   acknowledging we can't make it without God;
N   never giving up on God's purpose for our marriage;
T   talking to God every day and every night in our marriage;
I   interested in what God's Word says about marriage; and
C   celebrating the wonderful gift of *holy* matrimony in Christ."

So… if asked, are you *still* romantic? I hope your answer is a resounding… *with God, far more than the beginning!*

A Poem of Romance

Husbands and wives, if you desire a marriage
that's thriving and alive, here's a poem on
romance that may keep your union on the rise.

Husbands and wives,
God's desire for you
To love and live as one, and not as two.
Never let your romantic waters run dry.
Keep the fountain flowing by giving romance a try.
Let your romance be better than
anything you can rub on,
put on, shake up, or drink;

And... unleash those bottled-up feelings,
Before you go on the blink!
Use romance to enhance the love you already share,
So there'll be no need to seek it elsewhere.
When you're romantic, know that
your spouse is going to smile.
If you don't believe me, I dare you try it for a while.

"Therefore a man shall leave his father and his mother and hold fast to his wife, and they shall be one flesh' (Genesis 21:24).

"Let your fountains be blessed, and rejoice with the wife of your youth, a lovely deer, a graceful doe. Let her breasts fill you at all times with delight; be intoxicated always in her love" (Proverbs 5:18-19).

"The husband should give to his wife her conjugal rights, and like wise the wife to her husband" (1 Corinthians 7:3).

"I am my beloved's and my beloved is mine; he grazes among the lilies" (Song of Solomon 6:3).

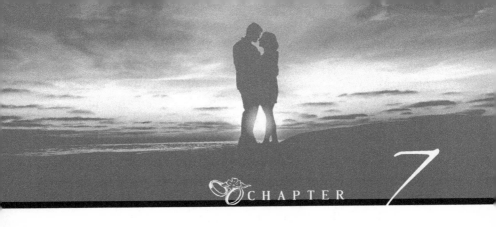

CHAPTER 7

Marital Miracle Moments
(M&M Moments)

hough many years have passed since we said I do, my husband and I have begun to look at our marriage as a product of God's amazing grace for His purpose and glory. Through it all: the ups and downs, hits and misses, good times and bad times, God through His miraculous love has always provided extra special moments in our marriage. We call these extra special times, our Marital Miracle Moments, or our M&M Moments. You may identify them in another way, but they can still be just as meaningful. I believe every marriage contains them, recognized or not.

Unfortunately, sometimes those M&M Moments may come about as a result of hardship and pain, which can occur within a marriage. For instance, a hardship may consist of one spouse becoming ill, and the other is given the strength and endurance to see them through. The

M&M Moment comes as a result of God dispensing His sustaining grace to care for and help meet the needs of the other spouse, directly or indirectly. Surely, being there 100% to support a spouse is an amazing and powerful work of God. I'm reminded what the Apostle Paul said: "But he said to me, 'My grace is sufficient for you, for my power is made perfect in weakness' " (2 Corinthians 12: 9).

Although there have been many, I remember a very special M&M Moment when my husband was there for me more than 100% to help care for a love one. God through His amazing grace had given me the opportunity to be conservator to one of my precious aunts, who (because of health issues) became helpless in the struggles she was facing. Being that she lived in Northern California, while we lived in Southern California, we had to make many trips to her home. This would consist of traveling up and around steep mountains, sometimes in hard rainy weather, snow, and fog so thick that one had to drive using their very wits. Since I had no experience in driving in such weather, I needed someone to help me. God did. He gave me a husband who was willing to support me in driving as many times as needed.

Finally, there came a time when I had to petition the courts for my aunt's relocation to our home. This made it more of an extensive process and hardship, in that we were to travel back and forth many more times. But despite the process, God was still on our side, having the Judge to grant our request.

Because I was still working, and my husband was retired, many times the care of my aunt fell on him. He never wavered in that care. Today, I thank God for having a spouse who was/is willing to make "my cause his cause" in love, support, and caring. So, husbands and wives, at all costs, I encourage you to be thankful for your spouse. Be there for them through the good times and the challenging ones. Surely, it was God's grace that carried us through, and that same grace is available for you.

These M&M moments also occurred when it was obvious to us that God stepped in and changed *us,* or the situation completely around. I shall never forget the time I was in the hospital in labor with our third child. Sadly, my husband had to work during that time. But I'm grateful the Lord still *had me* in His loving care. After being examined by a nurse, I asked timidly, "Is everything okay?" The nurse nodded as to say, "Yes," and immediately left the room. Shortly afterwards, another nurse came in and asked if I had been examined. My replied again was, "Yes." Given my response, she also began to leave. As she was walking to the door, she suddenly stopped, turned, and said in a very loving tone, "We don't usually check behind other nurses, but I'll just take a look."

During her examination, she discovered our baby was in distress with the umbilical cord wrapped around its neck three times, causing choking with each contraction. All praises to God, the nurse didn't leave my side, keeping her hand positioned for two hours between our baby's neck and the umbilical cord to help save her life. I truly believe, if the Spirit of the Lord hadn't moved that nurse to examine me a second time, the outcome could have been devastating! My husband and I are grateful that God stepped in (by having that second nurse to *step back in*) and changed that situation for the better. Grateful our daughter was delivered safely in that M&M Moment.

Also, if a spouse had done wrong or made a mistake, and the other forgives him/her, this is considered an M&M Moment in our eyes. As you may realize, forgiveness is something that we cannot do ourselves; it requires a work of God. We must pray, pray, and pray more all through the day, in hopes of maintaining a spirit of forgiveness. For my husband and I can attest, *it takes a willingness to submit to God's will for Him to do the work in our hearts to forgive*; just as he did on that early 2017 November morning.

We've also experienced some M&M Moments coming about with a bit of humor. There was a time when we were literally down to our last penny, and I had hoped to do some washing while my husband was at work. At that time, we didn't have a washing machine. While sweeping the living room floor one morning, I prayed and asked God for two dollars ($2.00). Yes, just two dollars, since that was all needed to use the washer up the street. I tell you, God sent someone by that very day and gave me exactly two dollars! I was tickled and amazed! That person had no idea I had just prayed and asked God for that amount. Afterwards, I remember thinking, "Wow, I should have asked for more!" Lord knows, we could have used it! Still, I was grateful, He gave me what I had asked for: two dollars. Won't He do it?

Although there were many times we were blind to what was happening, we now see that God was performing M&M Moments every day. For example, when God took the pity out of my pity party, that was an M&M Moment for us. As I look back, I can see the miracle/s God did in my heart and my husband's as well. God was beginning to change me so that I could see Him (GOD) for who He is. When He made me aware of how I was using my injury to control my husband, that too was an M&M Moment that brought a new outlook in our marriage. Not only that, but being awakened to the danger of "will waring" was another major M&M Moment.

Husbands and wives, also be mindful, things do not have to happen on a grand scale to be considered an

M&M Moment. When you're sensitive to the guidance of the Holy Spirit, you will begin to notice them, big or small; for it is He that makes the moment obvious. For instance, M&M Moments can be as simple as one spouse going on a trip and the other calls just to make sure they've arrived safely, which can be a really extra special moment of love and caring.

Some M&M Moments also can be as special as opening a car door, pulling out a chair, and holding hands, not to mention a needed embrace. Some might say, "Those small gestures are not considered miracles." I can't help but agree; in and of themselves, they are not. But what God did in the heart of your spouse—*was.* Sometimes the miracles happen on the inside and are reflected on the outside. If you haven't been receiving gestures of love as such, and now God has moved in your spouse's heart to do those "kind" things for you—again, that's an M&M Moment in our book. For miracles of God's love and care comes in many ways, especially when it involves the heart. Hopefully, you know or will come to know God as the "miracle heart specialist."

I declare, if it wasn't for the miracle of God's mercy and grace, we don't know where we would be today. How God took two very flawed, imperfect, and broken young people from the rural Delta of Mississippi from the cotton fields, and still maintaining them in holy matrimony is indeed humbling; how He picked us up and turned our marriage around for His glory will always be a miraculous act in our eyes. We give Him the utmost praise for awakening us to the sovereignty of His sustaining power. In spite of our ignorance, God never left our side.

Truly, being awakened to the sovereignty of God is an M&M Moment that changed the course and flow of our marriage. When we decided to give our marriage to

God and ask Him to control us, that's when we began to recognize His amazing love, provision, protection, covering, and control in all situations, which can be moments like no other! I'm reminded: "In him we have obtained an inheritance, having been predestined according to the purpose of him who works all things according to the counsel of his will," (Ephesians 1:11). My husband Harvest and I can honestly say, there have been M&M Moments of God's sovereignty and intervention in our marriage that caused us to fall on our knees and say, "Ah! Lord, thank You!"

Conclusion

In the *Sacred and Intimate Lives of Husbands and Wives,* we see that in the beginning God created the heavens and the earth. God also created man and gave him a helper fit for him. These two became one in holy matrimony by God *Himself.* Today, men and women are still being united in marriage under the biblical concept of "What therefore God has joined together, let not man separate" (Mark 10:9). Hopefully, you can now be certain that God instituted, approves, and honors this sacred and intimate covenant between husbands and wives.

I hope you realize that God established marriage for His purpose and not yours. It is a tool for Him; an instrument to demonstrate His sacrificial and unconditional love; and a light in the world to encourage men, women, boys, and girls toward salvation in Him through Christ Jesus the Lord. Also, I hope you appreciate all that God has done to lay the foundation through Him.

In light of God's sovereignty, I hope you will recognize Him as the Authority in your union. I hope you realize your union was not an accident; it was providentially arranged by God and is a precious gift from Him; His to keep together, but not without two willing hearts. You have a role to play.

Finally, after reading the helpful hints and scriptures

in this book, I hope you will become awakened to the moment by moment need for God in your marriage, and aware of the many miracles He provides. I hope this book encouraged you to embrace your marriage as God designed, and let it be reflective of His glory, love, and purpose through you.

My husband and I thank God for placing the love in our hearts for each other. But most importantly, we thank Him for placing His love in "two hearts" that became "one" in Him for His glory.

A Prayer for Marriages

Dear Lord,

*First, I thank and love You because of who You are. You are Lord. I pray for **all marriages** that You have joined together, and for those that are coming together in Your name. I pray they will recognize You as Lord of their union, praying their eyes will become open to make You front, head, and center.*

*I pray for those **anticipating marriage**, the **newly married**, and those **married a significant amount of years**. I pray they will come to know Your marriage plan better for their lives, and embrace it whole heartily, glorifying You in it.*

*I pray for those **unequally yoke marriages**, that they may come to accept Your salvation, love, and truth; that the saved husband might influence the wife to salvation, or the saved wife might lead the unsaved husband to faith in You by her conduct and love for You.*

*I pray for **"those"** whose marriages have been broken by divorce. I pray they will not give up on marriage. If there is unforgiveness Lord, I pray forgiveness takes precedence over any ill-will, hurt, and heartache. I also pray that each individual of that parted union will find strength and grace to carry on in You.*

79

I further pray for the "ones" whose marriages are no longer because of the death of a spouse. I pray for the comfort of the widowed spouses to hold on and keep depending on You.

Lastly, I pray that all spouses grow to use their marriage as a ministry to reflect and be a witness to the world of Your sacrificial love, grace, and mercy, leading others to salvation in You.

Now, I pray that You will help my husband Harvest and I to continue to look to You for strength and wisdom to go forward in our marriage.

I thank You, as I pray to always appreciate and embrace the sacredness and intimacy of the marriage journey, as designed in Your Word; and as reflected in **Sacred and Intimate Lives of Husbands and Wives,** *for Your glory in Jesus blessed name, Amen.*

About the Author

Hertistine is a resident of Los Angeles, California, where she lives with her loving husband of 43 years. She is the grateful mother of four children and grandmother of four. She grew up in the church and has come to love and appreciate the Lord. Hertistine believes marriage can be all it's meant to be when it's done according to God's plan. She gives Him all the glory for her life, and understands it is He who has guided her every step of the way.

Being raised in a Christian family, consisting of seven brothers and five sisters, her first role model for marriage and family were her mom and dad. She often observed their interactions. Hertistine saw that despite the trials and challenges of everyday living–raising twelve children, keeping food on the table, and finding time for themselves– her parent's love never wavered. She noticed how they were growing in love and respect for one another and also for the Lord.

On many levels, this gave her hope to one day have a spouse of like faith, and one that would love and adore her with the kind she witnessed from her parents. She is grateful God fulfilled her desire by giving her a spouse that not only loves her but loves Him more. She will be the first to admit, being in a marriage a significant amount of years has not always been smooth sailing. It has definitely had its share of ups and downs. But through it all, she declares and affirms, it was God who has kept them together loving, surviving, and thriving.

After marriage, Hertistine and her husband decided to pursue her dream of becoming a teacher. Thanks be to God, she is an alumnus of California State University Dominquez Hills, with a Bachelor's Degree in Human Services. She is also a retired preschool teacher from the Los Angeles Unified School District. On her blog, she is a writer of poems, short stories, and inspirational pieces on expressing gratitude in everything; in spite of experiencing various life issues. She is also the author of the book, *Something to Thank About from A to Z.* (xulonpress.com., amazon.com., and BarnesandNoble.com.)

Follow her on Facebook, Twitter, and her blog, keeponthanking.com.